FABERGÉ EGGS

Imperial Russian Fantasies

Introduction and Commentaries by
Christopher Forbes
Foreword by Armand Hammer
Photographs by Larry Stein

Harry N. Abrams, Inc., Publishers, New York

The line drawings for the catalog raisonné
of Fabergé Imperial Eggs were made especially
for this book by Lydia Gershey

Editor: Darlene Geis
Copy Editor: Charles W. Ervin
Designer: Gilda Kuhlman

Fifth Printing, 1983

Library of Congress Catalog Card Number: 79-55505
International Standard Book Number: 0-8109-2227-4

Photograph of the Coronation Egg by Peter MacDonald

Photograph of the Caucasus Egg courtesy of The Matilda
Geddings Gray Foundation Collection. All other eggs
in this book are from the FORBES Magazine Collection

Printed and bound in Japan

"Glittering Baubles Made
for a Czar"

The egg, perfect in form and carrying within it a new life, has been a universal symbol of rebirth for thousands of years. In Imperial Russia, where the Orthodox Christian Easter celebrating the Resurrection of Christ was the most important holiday of the year, gaily decorated eggs were exchanged with the glad tidings, "Christ Is Risen!" It remained for the Romanov Czars to raise this charming custom to the level of imperial luxury. And Peter Carl Fabergé, jeweler extraordinary, was the guiding genius responsible for these ultimate Easter eggs, aptly described by Rita Reif, antiques editor of *The New York Times*, as "glittering baubles made for a Czar." As "eggs" they are perhaps the most extravagant expression of a centuries-old tradition; as objects they mark one of the crowning achievements of the art of the goldsmith and the jeweler.

Fabergé was only twenty-four years old in 1870, when he took control of his father's small but moderately successful jewelry business in the Russian Imperial capital, St. Petersburg (now Leningrad). The family was descended from French Protestants who had fled France when Louis XIV revoked the Edict of Nantes in 1685, eventually coming to rest in Russia more than a century later. The young Fabergé was educated in Germany and learned the family trade by apprenticing under several of the leading Continental goldsmiths of the day. He also visited the major state and royal collections in Rome, Venice, Florence, London, Paris, Dresden, Munich, and Berlin.

After his return to St. Petersburg, Peter Carl Fabergé devoted the next dozen years to reorganizing and expanding the firm with the assistance of his gifted younger brother, Agathon. He had a definite objective in mind, one upon which he was prepared to risk the family's business. He decided to challenge the prevailing criterion that based the importance of a piece of jewelry upon the quantity of precious materials that it combined. In the House of Fabergé the emphasis was shifted from carat content to craftsmanship and creativity.

Fabergé supervised some of the most talented craftsmen that could be found, although he himself never actually worked on any of the pieces which bear the family name. The firm was divided into several workshops, each under the direction of a workmaster specializing in a particular aspect of the craft. Conventional jewelry, table silver, hardstone carvings, old Russian pieces in the so-called Pan-Slavic style, and translucently enamelled *objets de luxe* in the more European taste all were created under the guidance of specialists. Fabergé's particular genius lay in his ability to inspire each of these artists and artisans to work together with his designers and miniaturists, creating the incredible fantasy pieces that have brought enduring fame to the House of Fabergé.

The two workmasters most involved with the fabled Easter eggs were Michael Evlampievich Perchin and Henrik Wigström. Perchin was a prodigy who in 1886 at the age of twenty-six became the leading workmaster for the House of Fabergé, producing many of its Imperial eggs. Unlike most of his colleagues, who were of Scandinavian origin, Perchin was a native Russian. All the signed Imperial Easter eggs made before 1903, the year he ceased working for the firm, are stamped with his mark, *M.П.* (M.P.). Henrik Wigström, a Swedish Finn two years younger than Perchin, worked as his assistant for several years and eventually succeeded him. All the signed Imperial eggs produced after 1903 bear Wigström's mark, *H.W.*; however, only about half of the eggs are stamped. It is conceivable, therefore, that other workmasters may have been involved in producing some of the later eggs.

Objects from the House of Fabergé made of precious metals, in addition to being stamped by the workmaster responsible, also usually have Russian assay marks. These include the stamps indicating metal purity and city of origin. Metal purity was measured in *zolotniks*; there are about four in one carat. Fourteen-carat gold was therefore stamped 56 *zolotniks*, eighteen-carat gold 72 *zolotniks,* and so on. Silver just above the sterling standard of 92.5 percent pure silver was at least 91 *zolotniks,* although more frequently lesser grades were used because they were better for enamelling. Prior to the reign of Nicholas II, each major Russian city had used its own metal mark. For St. Petersburg it was a pair of anchors crossed, and for Moscow, St. George and the dragon. After 1896 a national mark began to supercede the regional ones. This was the profile of a woman wearing the traditional *kokoshnik* headdress and is usually called simply the *kokoshnik.*

The small jelly-bean-sized eggs, a selection of which are illustrated in this book, bear the marks of a number of workmasters of varied nationalities, including Johan Victor Aarne (Finnish), Fedor Afanassiev (Russian), August Frederick Hollming (Finnish), Erik Kollin (Swedish Finn), G. Lundell (Swedish Finn), J.F. Okerblöm (Russian), Knut Oscar Pihl (Swedish Finn), Alfred Thielemann (German), and Alexander Tillander. The most important among this group was Erik Kollin, a goldsmith whose replicas of Scythian gold objects attracted the favorable attention of Czarevich Alexander, who was to become Czar Alexander III.

On March 1, 1881, Alexander II's carriage was rocked by a bomb blast. Uninjured, the Czar descended to help the wounded. A second bomb exploded, blowing off one of his legs. He died shortly thereafter, surrounded by his family in the Winter Palace. He was succeeded by his energetic and autocratic eldest son, Alexander III. Although it is known that the new Czar admired the Fabergé replicas of the Scythian treasure, it is not known how Fabergé came to produce the first surprise Easter egg for his sovereign. One story has it that Fabergé was asked by the Czar to create an ingenious Easter present to divert his wife, Maria, and relieve her gloom after the assassination of his father. However, since the practical Danish-born Czarina hated her pro-German father-in-law, it seems unlikely that she brooded over his premature demise. Another story has it that Fabergé had the First Imperial Egg created on his own initiative in order to gain favor with the Czar. Unless additional clarifying documentation comes to light, theories on the origin of the First Imperial Egg are mere speculation. Even the date of its creation is uncertain. The year 1886, when Perchin became a Fabergé workmaster, would seem the most likely; however, 1884 and 1885 have also been suggested. Nevertheless, what is undisputed is that the sovereigns were pleased enough to make a Fabergé surprise egg an Easter tradition.

Nicholas II, who came to the throne in 1894 and was in so many respects an inadequate Czar in comparison with his father, surpassed him in at least one area—he presented not only his wife, Alexandra Feodorovna, with a Fabergé egg each year, but his mother, Maria, as well. Thus, between 1886 and 1916 a total of 53 eggs was presented to the two Czarinas. The eggs for the fateful year 1917, if they were ever completed, were not delivered.

Easter eggs from Fabergé were not confined to the Imperial family. A series of eggs almost rivaling those created for the Czarinas was made for Barbara Bazanov Kelch, an heiress whose wealth came from property in the Urals. Other major fantasy eggs were executed for the Emanuel Nobel family, whose fortune was derived from the manufacture of dynamite and from Siberian oil, for Prince Felix Yussupov, and for the Duchess of Marlborough, née Consuelo Vanderbilt. Smaller surprise eggs and egg charms by the hundreds were available along with other sumptuous *objets* in any of the five Fabergé shops. The egg form itself was used for various functional articles such as parasol and cane handles, bonbonnières, vodka cups, and hand seals.

One such object, the egg-shaped Hvidore seal, is the only piece of Fabergé FORBES Magazine acquired directly from a member of the Imperial family, Prince Vassili Romanov, a grandson of Czar Alexander III. Other pieces have passed through the hands of a variety of owners, including such diverse personalities as J. P. Morgan, King Farouk of Egypt, Dr. Armand Hammer, and President Franklin D. Roosevelt. In the foreword to the first catalogue of the FORBES Magazine Collection, Malcolm S. Forbes recalled his earliest exposure to the art of Fabergé:

> When very young, I read with horrified fascination an abundantly illustrated volume on World War I. Its chapter about the Russian Revolution and the massacre of the Romanov Family included a picture of a Fabergé Imperial Egg to illustrate the pre-War extravagance of Russia's rulers.

In the early 1960s he began acquiring Fabergé's masterpieces, and the collection was unveiled in 1967 to commemorate the golden anniversary of the founding of FORBES Magazine.

The first major egg Forbes acquired was that created for Consuelo, Duchess of Marlborough. This was soon followed by two Imperial eggs, the Orange Tree Egg and the Renaissance Egg. The death of shipping magnate Lansdell K. Christie brought to FORBES the Spring Flowers, Chanticleer, and Kelch Hen Eggs from The Metropolitan Museum of Art in New York, where they were on loan. The Fifteenth Anniversary Egg, perhaps the most personal of all those created for the Imperial family, was purchased shortly thereafter. The Cross of St. George Egg was acquired in the early 1970s. The First Egg and the Resurrection Egg were added to the collection in time to be included in the revised catalogue of the collection published in the fall of 1978. The foreword to this catalogue ended with the following paragraph:

> History is not without its amusing ironies. In September 1917, one month before the Soviets seized power in Russia, B.C. Forbes published the first issue of FORBES Magazine. Sixty-one years later, the "Capitalist Tool," as FORBES is known, owns only two fewer of Fabergé's Imperial Eggs than the Soviet Government.

Six months after that was written, the gap was closed by Malcolm Forbes's purchase of two of the most renowned Fabergé Easter creations of all, the Coronation and Lilies-of-the-Valley Eggs.

Christopher Forbes

My Quest for the Fabergé Eggs

As an art collector for the past sixty years, during which I have assembled four renowned collections, it is indeed a privilege to write a preface to this book, which presents some of the most spectacular achievements of Peter Carl Fabergé, a goldsmith of consummate artistry and ingenuity, appropriately called the "Benvenuto Cellini of Czarist Russia."

After spending nine years in Russia, from 1921 to 1930, as the first American to do business in that country following the Bolshevik Revolution, I wrote a book entitled *The Quest of the Romanoff Treasure.* In it I told the story of how my brother Victor and I had come to garner, during our residence in Moscow, a stunning collection of art treasures, including intimate objects of the Romanov family. Among these was a great collection by the Court Jeweler, Peter Carl Fabergé, including many of the fabulous Easter eggs exchanged by the members of the Imperial family.

It all happened as follows: In 1921 I graduated from Columbia University with a medical degree. While studying medicine, I had to take over my father's small, almost insolvent, pharmaceutical company. I ran the business during the day and studied at night. By the time I graduated, the company was worth several million dollars. While waiting for my internship, I decided to help fight the typhus epidemic then raging in Russia in the aftermath of the Revolution by heading up my own field hospital there. However, after my arrival I realized that the massive famine was an even greater killer than typhus. To help the starving

Russians, I arranged for the first barter agreement with the USSR by bringing one million tons of wheat from the United States in exchange for furs, hides, and other commodities. My funds from the pharmaceutical business had made this transaction possible. Lenin, whom I came to know as a friend, awarded me mining and trading concessions.

After nine incredible years in Russia, upon the advent of the Stalin era, my brother Victor and I sold out. An important part of the agreement for the sale of our interests was the permission granted us to take out of Russia our entire collection of art treasures. Among these were eighteenth-century fabrics, shimmering with gold and silver threads, glassware and porcelain made in the Czar's private Imperial Porcelain Factory, icons, and paintings by old masters. Included among the priceless jeweled pieces we had obtained was a collection of fifteen Easter eggs executed in the workshops of Fabergé. We had first heard of Fabergé's eggs in conversations with officials of the Antiquariat, a division of the Ministry of Foreign Trade. We were able to convince Mr. Anastas Mikoyan, then minister of foreign trade, to have the Antiquariat sell us some of the Fabergé eggs. Later, a number of the eggs were sent to Berlin, where we and others had the opportunity to purchase them.

The liquidation of our Romanov collection, over a period of many years, was accomplished through the Hammer Galleries in New York City and in department stores throughout the United States. This was one way of realizing part of our investment in the Soviet Union. Wherever the sales took place, the Fabergé eggs were a great center of attraction, even though difficult to sell in the middle of the Depression.

Our collection of Easter eggs covered a period starting with the First Imperial Egg of 1886. We also acquired the Caucasus Egg (1893), the Renaissance Egg (1894), the Danish Palace Egg (1895), the Egg with Revolving Miniatures (1896), the Pelican Egg (1897), the Pansy Egg (1899), the Pine Cone Egg (1900), the Swan Egg (1906), the Czarevich Egg (1912), the Napoleonic Egg (1912), the Grisaille Egg (1914), and the Red Cross Egg with Portraits (1915). In addition, the collection contained the Kelch Hen Egg (1898), and a similar egg of carved lapis lazuli mounted in gold, as well as the Jade Chest Egg.

I believe art can contribute to understanding among peoples. Rembrandt's *Juno* does not speak Dutch. She speaks a universal language to all of us. The arts unite mind with heart and provide a common ground for the enjoyment and appreciation of beauty and perfection. Peter Carl Fabergé's masterpieces were the delight of the Romanov Court, the nobility, and the wealthy in Russia and in Europe. Here in this striking volume, *Fabergé Eggs: Imperial Russian Fantasies,* they are presented in a way that will bring enjoyment to countless lovers of art and beauty everywhere with their splendor and virtuosity.

Armand Hammer

SPRING FLOWERS EGG

Height: 3½"
Marks: MP (Michael Perchin), 56, crossed anchors,
FABERGÉ
Presented by Czar Alexander III to his wife, Maria
Feodorovna, c. 1890

Executed in the Louis XV style, the Spring Flowers Egg, like the other early Imperial Easter eggs, is smaller than the later, more extravagant creations. The gold shell is enamelled a deep strawberry red on an elaborately engraved or guilloche ground and encased in a rococo gold cage. Encircling the egg from bottom to top, a band of rose diamonds terminates in a diamond-set clasp, completing the decoration of the egg itself.

The fluted bowenite base, also banded with rose diamonds, rests on a circlet of fretted gold scrolling. A short gold pedestal joins the egg to the base.

SPRING FLOWERS EGG, in original case

Height of case: 5⅜"
Stamped: FABERGÉ/St. Petersburg, Moscow, London

The Spring Flowers Egg is shown here in its
original presentation box. Executed in white
maple, covered with pale cream velvet, and lined
with white silk stamped in gold with "Imperial
Warrant of the House of Fabergé," this case is
typical of Fabergé's sensibility to aesthetic detail.
It is not just a box. It, too, is an egg—a plain
outer shell hinting at the luxury of the treasure
within.

SPRING FLOWERS EGG, open

Height of basket: 1½"
Unmarked

A gentle twist of the clasp, and the shell of the Spring Flowers Egg parts to reveal the surprise from which its name is derived—an exquisite basket of spring wood anemones. A dazzling bouquet of flowers, consisting of white chalcedony petals with demantoid garnet centers and engraved gold stems, blossoms amidst translucent green enamel leaves. The basket of open Gothic design is wrought of platinum set with rose diamonds and can be easily lifted from the gold pedestal on which it rests.

After the long Russian winter the appearance of the first flowers of spring was especially welcome. Fabergé used a similar surprise in another larger and more elaborate egg also created for Czarina Maria Feodorovna in 1913, the rock crystal and diamond Winter Egg.

CORONATION EGG

Height: 5"
Length of coach: 3¹¹⁄₁₆"
Marks: MP (Michael Perchin), 56, crossed anchors
Presented by Czar Nicholas II to his wife, Alexandra Feodorovna, 1897

Certainly the best known and most frequently reproduced of all the Imperial Easter eggs, the Coronation Egg may indeed be the masterpiece of the House of Fabergé. The egg itself is enamelled a lustrous translucent yellow on an engraved gold starburst field trellised with gold bands of laurel. Opaque black-enamelled Imperial eagles set with diamonds are perched at each intersection of the trellis. Finial and terminal table diamonds, surrounded by brilliants set in engraved gold mounts, cover the red enamelled crowned cypher of the Czarina Alexandra and the date, 1897 (the first Easter after the coronation).

The surprise inside this egg is an exquisite miniature of the coronation coach, faithful to the original in every detail. George Stein, a former coachmaker turned goldsmith, spent fifteen months under Perchin's supervision fabricating this incredible fantasy. The red lacquer and velvet upholstery of the original are replicated in a deep red enamel, the gilt wood frame in chased gold, the iron wheel rims in platinum, and the glass windows in etched rock crystal. An Imperial crown in rose diamonds surmounts the carriage. The interior is enamelled with powder blue curtains and turquoise blue ceiling. A small gold hook is the only remaining evidence of the miniature diamond egg that once hung inside the carriage.

On the same Easter when Nicholas presented to Alexandra this extraordinary remembrance of their coronation, she in turn gave him a gold box similarly enamelled and set with Imperial eagles and the Czar's cypher in brilliant-cut diamonds. These companion gifts are now reunited in one collection.

CHANTICLEER EGG

Height: 10⅞" closed, 12⅝" open
Marks: MP (Michael Perchin), 56 kokoshnik,
FABERGÉ
Presented by Czar Nicholas II to his mother, Maria
Feodorovna, c. 1903

A dazzling little golden chanticleer, naturalistically chased and enamelled in yellow, blue, and green, its feathers set with diamonds, emerges from beneath a gold grille to crow the hour—head bobbing, wings flapping, even the tiny beak moving. The roost of this proud cockerel is the second largest Imperial Easter egg created by the House of Fabergé. Only the Uspensky Cathedral Egg of 1904 stands taller.

The egg and the four concave panels of the base are enamelled a brilliant sapphire blue on a wavy guilloche gold ground. Foliated gold swags hang from ribbons of gold that encircle the grille atop the egg. A band of seed pearls bordered with gold foliage horizontally circumscribes the egg. The crystal-covered white enamel clock face has a gold bezel that is also rimmed with seed pearls. The clock face is decorated with pale green enamel garlands and blue numerals.

The large panels of the pedestal are applied with gold armorial motifs symbolizing Music and Medicine. Similar motifs reflecting these special interests of the Czarina Maria Feodorovna decorate many of the eggs made for her after the death of Alexander III. The fluted shaft and small corner panels of the base are enamelled pale blue and mounted with elaborate two-colored gold motifs. At the back of the egg a pierced grille conceals the clockwork mechanism, wound by a large silver key.

The egg is similar to the Cuckoo Egg presented to Czarina Alexandra in 1900. The earlier egg is enamelled violet and decorated in the Louis XV rococo style, while the larger and mechanically more sophisticated Chanticleer Egg is in the Louis XVI, Neoclassical style.

This egg, the Gatchina Palace Egg, the Rose Trellis Egg, as well as several of those made for mining heiress Barbara Kelch, appeared in Paris prior to the sales from the Imperial treasure begun by the Soviet government in the mid-1920s.

EGG BONBONNIÈRE

Height: 1⅞"
Marks: HW (Henrik Wigström), 88 kokoshnik

This delicate little egg is actually a box that might well have been used for holding the sugared pastilles so popular at the turn of the century. Here a gilt-silver shell is enamelled a translucent white underpainted with sepia moss agate. Chased gold laurel swags punctuated with rubies encircle the lower half of the egg. The diamond-shaped areas of the shell delimited by these symmetrical swags are enamelled a robin's egg blue and applied with gold trelliswork with rose diamond quatrefoils at the interstices. The hinged cover, also in blue and white enamel, is applied with gold bows and foliate motifs centered with rose diamonds. Ruby-headed pins hold three gold rosettes to the lower half of the egg.

For all its small size, this bonbonnière is a technically challenging example of Fabergé workmanship.

FIRST IMPERIAL EGG

Length: 2½"
Diameter of yolk: 1⁹⁄₁₆"
Length of hen: 1³⁄₈"
Unmarked
Presented by Czar Alexander III to his wife, Maria Feodorovna, c. 1886

This simple gold egg inaugurated the Imperial Easter custom of presenting jewelled Fabergé surprise eggs to the Czarina. Enamelled matte white to resemble a hen's egg, the shell opens to reveal its surprise—a gold hen with ruby eyes nestled within the dull-gold yolk on a nest of chased yellow-gold straw. Originally, fitted inside the hen was a tiny replica of the Imperial crown from which was suspended a miniature ruby egg. Sad to say, these two additional surprises have been lost.

The First Imperial Egg was probably inspired by a French eighteenth-century ivory surprise egg in the collection of the Czarina's father, King Christian IX of Denmark. After being offered by various dealers, the First Imperial Egg appeared at a London auction in 1934 and was bought by Sir Arthur Svenson-Taylor for only £80 (about $400 at the time).

ORANGE TREE EGG

Height: 10½" closed, 11¾" open
Marks: FABERGÉ, 1911
Presented by Czar Nicholas II to his mother, Maria Feodorovna, 1911

This miniature topiary orange tree sprouts carved nephrite leaves from gold branches. Tiny white-enamelled gold blossoms with diamond centers are intermingled with ripening oranges made of amethysts, citrines, pale sapphires, and champagne diamonds.

The tree is rooted in a tub of white chalcedony overlaid by a gold trellis and mounted with natural pearl finials at its four corners. Green enamelled laurel swags are pinned to the tub with cabochon rubies, which are used also on the feet, centered between small gold-mounted rose diamonds. The tub rests on a nephrite base and is protected by a chain of gold leaves enamelled translucent green and interspersed with pearls. The chain swings from nephrite posts spirally banded with chased gold and topped with seed pearl finials.

If all this remarkable detail were not enough, the turning of a particular orange causes a portion of the foliage at the top of the tree to rise. A miniature feathered nightingale emerges, warbles sweetly as it dances on its perch, then automatically disappears. Dr. Everett Fahy, Director of the Frick Collection in New York, observed in his essay in the Fabergé catalogue of the FORBES Magazine collection:

> It brings to mind a passage from W. B. Yeats' "Sailing to Byzantium":

> But such a form as Grecian goldsmiths make
> Of hammered gold and gold enamelling
> To keep a drowsy Emperor awake
> Or set upon a golden bough to sing
> To lords and ladies of Byzantium
> Of what is past or passing, or to come.

> Yeats added a note to his poem, saying, "I have read somewhere that in the Emperor's palace at Byzantium was a tree made of gold and silver and artificial birds that sang." One might add that just such a tree with a singing bird was made in 1911 for Nicholas II of Russia.

KELCH HEN EGG

Length: 3½"
Height with stand: 3⅝"
Length of hen: 1⅜"
Height of easel: 1⅞"
Marks: MP (Michael Perchin), 56 kokoshnik, FABERGÉ
Presented by Alexander Ferdinandovich Kelch to his wife, the Siberian mining heiress, Barbara Bazanov, 1898

This egg is a more elaborate variation on the theme of the First Imperial Egg. The eggshell itself, which is enamelled a rich strawberry on a guilloche gold ground and banded with rose diamonds, bears no resemblance to a real egg. But the yolk, enamelled matte yellow, and the glossy egg white are startlingly lifelike. The egg opens lengthwise to reveal the white and yolk, which in turn conceal a naturalistically enamelled gold hen nested in suede. A further surprise is hidden in the hen, which opens on a hinge concealed in its tail feathers. A tiny folding easel is tucked inside. The easel now holds a rose diamond frame with a miniature portrait of Czarevich Alexis in the uniform of the Imperial family's own Fourth Rifle Battalion of Guards. This was substituted for the original miniature of Barbara Bazanov Kelch, whose initials once glimmered under a table diamond on the end of the egg. They have now been replaced with a tiny photograph of Czar Nicholas II. These changes were probably made while the egg was in France in the 1920s.

The varicolored gold stand hung with floral swags set with diamonds is also not an original part of the egg. It was made either for King Farouk of Egypt, who owned the egg until the early 1950s, or for Liberian shipping magnate Lansdell K. Christie, whose widow sold the egg to FORBES in 1966.

SIX ORIGINAL FABERGÉ EGG CASES

Left to right, cases for the:

Renaissance Egg (8" long)
Cross of St. George Egg (7¼" high)
Duchess of Marlborough Egg (10" high)
Kelch Hen Egg (4½" long)
Fifteenth Anniversary Egg (8⅜" high)
Spring Flowers Egg (5⅜" high)

The four egg-shaped cases covered with pale velvet, now much faded and worn, are the original cases in which the Renaissance, Cross of St. George, Fifteenth Anniversary, and Spring Flowers Eggs came to the Imperial family.

In a ceremonious ritual that included instruction on the working of the surprise, Peter Carl Fabergé himself would deliver these handsome boxes and their priceless contents to the Czar. In later years when the Dowager Empress Maria Feodorovna did not spend Easter with her son and his family, old Fabergé would deliver her egg while his son, Eugène, brought the Czarina's to Nicholas II.

The larger of the two polished white maple boxes is the original case for the Duchess of Marlborough Egg. It is fitted with polished nickel handles for traveling. The Kelch Hen Egg fits snugly in its original case, as does its surprise hen seen here in its suede nest.

All of the cases have velvet covered recesses in which the egg is held firmly, while the lid and sides of the boxes are lined with padded white silk stamped in gold or black with the Imperial warrant of the House of Fabergé.

HVIDORE SEAL

Height: 2¼"
Marks: MP (Michael Perchin), FABERGÉ, 56,
crossed anchors
From the collection of the Czarina Maria Feodorovna
and her sister, Queen Alexandra of Great Britain

This hand seal is a fine example of Fabergé's use of the egg form to make unusual and amusing functional objects. The seal was pressed onto hot wax on communications sent from Hvidore, the villa owned by the Czarina and her sister.

The nephrite egg is enclosed in pierced gold scrollwork in the rococo style, similar to the mount of the Spring Flowers Egg. The wavy gold shaft terminates in a reed-and-leaf motif holding the circular carnelian matrix in which is cut the word HVIDORE. This inscription is explained by Prince Vassili Romanov, the grandson of Czar Alexander III, from whom this seal was acquired:

My late Grandmother, the Empress Dowager Maria Feodorovna and her sister Queen Alexandra bought a villa in 1907 outside Copenhagen with large gardens on to the seashore and named it HVIDORE which means "white ear" for a strip of beach that stuck out into the sea resembling an ear. So the seal has that name.

RENAISSANCE EGG

Length: 5¼"
Marks: MP (Michael Perchin), FABERGÉ, 56,
crossed anchors
Presented by Czar Alexander III to his wife, Maria
Feodorovna, 1894

This sumptuous egg of milky chalcedony was inspired by a sixteenth-century jewelled casket in the Grünes Gewölbe Museum which Fabergé knew from his student days in Dresden. Slightly truer to the egg shape than the earlier work, Fabergé's masterpiece is similarly trellised with opaque white enamel gold bands decorated with ruby-centered quatrefoils of rose diamonds. Renaissance-style foliate motifs brilliantly enamelled in translucent reds, greens, blues, and opaque white are set with diamonds and cabochon rubies. These decorations radiate from the red enamelled guilloche gold band bisecting the egg and surround the enamelled plaque surmounting the egg on which the date, 1894, is set in rose diamonds.

The egg rests on its side on a gold base with palmettes and flowers enamelled in translucent green and red against an opaque white enamel background. The casket is completed with gold loop handles that swing from chased gold lion masks.

The surprise, probably a large jewel once contained in the casket, is now lost. This was the last of the Imperial eggs made for Alexander III before his untimely death on November 1, 1894.

FIVE MINIATURE EASTER EGGS

Height: from ¾″ to 1⅛″
Marks: various workmasters

Miniature eggs were among the most popular items offered for sale at Fabergé's shops in St. Petersburg, Moscow, Odessa, Kiev, and London. On Easter morning the well-to-do would exchange precious egg charms such as these with the greeting "Christ Is Risen!" The sizes of the eggs pictured opposite, including their loops, range from ¾″ high for the auburn enamelled egg with the gold fleur-de-lys to 1¼″ for the wartime rhodonite egg mounted with a silver cannon executed by workmaster Alexander Thieleman.

The pink enamelled egg underpainted with sepia moss agate motifs and banded with rose diamonds is the work of Henrik Wigström and bears a family resemblance to his Bonbonnière on page 19. It comes from the collection of the late Princess Royal of Great Britain and was possibly a gift from her great aunt, Czarina Maria Feodorovna.

CAUCASUS EGG

Height: 3⅝", with stand 6⅛"
Marks: MP (Michael Perchin), 72, crossed anchors
Presented by Alexander III to his wife, Maria
Feodorovna, 1893. In the collection of The Matilda
Geddings Gray Foundation, New Orleans

This sumptuous egg in the Louis XV style is enamelled a translucent ruby red over a basket-weave guilloche gold ground. Four-color gold swags, together with pendants hanging from platinum bows set with rose diamonds, encircle the top and bottom of the egg. Four oval portals, one on each face of the egg, carry the numerals set in rose diamonds that make up the date 1893. Each numeral is framed by a laurel wreath set in rose diamonds, and the portals are rimmed with oriental pearls.

The surprise is revealed when each of the portals swings open to disclose four miniatures on ivory, painted by K. Kryitski. These depict the Imperial retreat at Abastouman in the Caucasus, the mountain residence of Grand Duke George Alexandrovich, the Czar's younger brother, who suffered from lung trouble and was thought to benefit from the high altitude. He died in 1899 at the age of twenty eight.

When the egg is held to a light, a portrait miniature of the tragic young Grand Duke that is set in the center of the egg can be seen through table diamonds framed with rose diamonds at the top and bottom of the egg. The elaborate gold wire stand is not original but was commissioned by the Hammer Galleries.

This was the last Imperial egg to be enamelled red. After the Czarevich's birth in 1904 the color was associated with his hemophilia, and so red became taboo. An exception was the red cross on the Red Cross Eggs of 1915.

RABBIT EGG

Height: 2", with stand 3⅜"
Length of rabbit: 1⅛"
Marks: MP (Michael Perchin), 56 kokoshnik

Neither an Imperial egg nor a piece specially commissioned by a titled or powerful client, this little surprise egg is typical of the charming fantasies that made shopping at Fabergé *de rigueur* for the beautiful people of the *belle époque*.

The egg is of silver gilt, enamelled translucent yellow on a wavy guilloche ground. The hinge is concealed in a rim of green gold acanthus leaves. The rabbit, crouched in a burrow of chased-gold grass, is carved of pink chalcedony and set with olivine eyes. The gold wire stand, perhaps of later manufacture, is set with a red enamelled Czarina Elizabeth I ruble dated 1756.

FIFTEENTH ANNIVERSARY EGG

Height: 5⅛", with stand 6¼"
Marks: FABERGÉ in blue enamel
Presented by Czar Nicholas II to his wife, Alexandra Feodorovna, 1911

The Fifteenth Anniversary Egg is the most personal of all the eggs created for the ill-fated Nicholas II and his wife, Alexandra. Portrayed in oval miniatures on ivory by Vassily Zuiev are the Czar, the Czarina, and their children, Grand Duchesses Olga, Tatiana, Marie, Anastasia, and Czarevich Alexis.

Additional rectangular miniatures depict in incredible detail the principle events of the reign through 1911. These include: The Alexander III Museum; The procession to Uspensky Cathedral; The opening of the Alexander III bridge in Paris; The Huis ten Bosch, The Hague; The reception for the members of the First State Duma at the Winter Palace, St. Petersburg; The unveiling of the monument commemorating the Bicentenary of the Battle of Poltava; The unveiling of the statue of Peter the Great at Riga; The moment of Coronation; The removal of the remains of the Saint Serafim Sarovski. The miniatures are set on a gold egg which is segmented with translucent green enamelled laurel trellising tied with rose diamonds. The portraits are framed with rose diamonds and centered in fields of translucent oyster-white enamel bordered with opaque white enamel.

Surmounting the egg is a table diamond under which appears the Czarina's crowned cypher in black enamel on a gold ground. This finial is framed in rose diamonds bordered by chased gold palmettes. The similarly bordered terminal is a Dutch rose-cut champagne-colored diamond weighing approximately five carats.

The dates of the Czar's wedding, 1894, and the fifteenth anniversary of his coronation, 1911, appear in roundels below the miniatures of the Imperial couple. The detachable gold stand is probably the original.

FISH CHARKA
filled with miniature eggs

Width: 3¼", including handle
Marks: MP (Michael Perchin), FABERGÉ, 56,
crossed anchors

Brimming with miniature Fabergé egg charms, this handsome gold *charka* looks like a fancy cup full of jelly beans. Six white- and red-gold fish with ruby eyes are applied to the surface of the gold bowl, which is chased to resemble flowing water. The sea motif is further reinforced with six gold scallop shells applied to the foot. The gold handle frames a Czarina Elizabeth I ruble that is dated 1756 and is mounted with a cabochon sapphire.

DUCHESS OF MARLBOROUGH EGG

Height: 9"
Marks: MP (Michael Perchin), 56 kokoshnik,
FABERGÉ, 1902
Made for Consuelo, Duchess of Marlborough, 1902

This egg has the unique distinction of being the only major Fabergé egg made for an American. Consuelo, Duchess of Marlborough, was born Consuelo Vanderbilt, daughter of W. K. Vanderbilt, whose socially ambitious wife forced her daughter to marry Winston Churchill's ducal cousin. The Duchess acquired the egg during a visit to Russia in 1902 when she and her husband were received by the Dowager Empress. It is possible that at this time the Duchess may have seen the Imperial Serpent Clock Egg, almost identical to this one but enamelled blue rather than pink.

The egg is bisected by a revolving band of opaque white enamel bordered with seed pearls and set with rose diamond numerals. A diamond-studded serpent marks the passing hours with his golden tongue. Garlands of roses in four colors of gold, hanging from rose diamond bows, encircle the egg. The chased gold handles terminate in rams' masks and the egg is crowned with a diamond-set pineapple finial.

Framed in the base are three translucent white enamel guilloche gold panels, two decorated with gold armorial trophies symbolizing Science and War and the third with the Duchess' coronet and cypher, CM, in rose diamonds. This egg and its Imperial precursor were inspired by urn clocks made in France during the reign of Louis XVI.

TWENTY-EIGHT MINIATURE EGGS

Height: from ¾" to 1¼"
Marks: various workmasters

The incredible imagination and versatility of Fabergé's workmasters are brilliantly displayed in this assortment of miniature egg charms. Materials range from gemstones and gold to silver and man-made hardstone, purpurine, to simple polished holly wood.

The largest little egg (measuring 1¼ inches) and the most elaborate of those pictured is the purpurine egg mounted with a black enamelled gold helmet of Her Majesty's Guard Lancers. Particularly fanciful are the plump gunmetal fish with fins and tail of gold and ruby eyes; the brightly enamelled gold lady bug by Michael Perchin; and Henrik Wigström's acorn of nephrite paved with rose diamonds. Extravagance is epitomised by Eric Kollin's egg encrusted entirely with rubies and Wigström's similar piece paved with rose diamonds and emeralds.

Special occasions are commemorated in these miniature baubles—the Coronation with Perchin's white-and-yellow banded egg set with the Imperial crown; the alliance with Great Britain with Lundell's white enamel egg painted with the Union Jack; and the awarding of the Cross of St. George with the unsigned lime enamel egg, chased and enamelled with the Cross of the Order.

Imagination, restrained luxury, and appropriately fine materials are the hallmarks of Fabergé's style, whether he was creating an Imperial Easter egg almost a foot tall or a tiny charm measuring less than an inch.

MINIATURE CHICK EGG

Height: 1"
Marks: Fedor Afanassiev

This delightful Easter fantasy measures only one inch in height, including its loop. The fluffy pink chick standing on his gold egg-shaped perch is naturalistically carved from amethystine quartz and set with rose diamond eyes.

Fedor Afanassiev, the workmaster whose mark is on this piece, specialized in small objects of fantasy. His workshop and that of Henrik Wigström produced most of the carved hardstone flowers and figurines which were among the most popular *objets d'art* that were created by the House of Fabergé.

FIVE MINIATURE EGG CHARMS

Height: from ¾″ to ⅞″
Marks: various workmasters

Three of these jelly-bean-sized charms have particularly strong Imperial themes. Perchin's three tiny eggs on one loop are enamelled in the Imperial colors of blue and red and the Czarina's favorite mauve. Afanassiev's contribution is enamelled the color of rich gold cloth with the black, double-headed Imperial eagle on the front. The back has bands of white, blue, and red, the colors of Imperial Russia. This charm may well have been created to commemorate the coronation of Nicholas II that took place in 1896.

The unsigned egg enamelled with the Red Cross reflects one of the interests of the Imperial family. The Czarina, her eldest daughters, her sister, and her mother-in-law all worked as nurses for the Red Cross during World War I. The Imperial eggs created for Alexandra and Maria Feodorovna in 1915 reflect in their decoration this dedication to the Red Cross. An almost identical miniature Red Cross Egg in the FORBES Magazine Collection is signed by August Hollming.

The other two egg charms are noteworthy, one for the exceptional quality of the miniature hatching chick, and the other for its Art Nouveau style, which is relatively rare in Fabergé's oeuvre.

SCENT FLACON EGG

Height: 1¼"
Marks: H.W. (Henrik Wigström), 56

Another functional egg, this miniature scent bottle was designed to be hung on a bracelet or neck chain, enabling the wearer to have a dab of perfume readily available.

The stopper, set with a moonstone, is surrounded by chased-gold palmettes. A similar motif, embellished with miniature garlands and swags set with diamonds, encircles the loop. The engraved gold shell is enamelled a delicate powder blue.

RESURRECTION EGG

Height: 3⅞"
Marks: MP (Michael Perchin), 56, crossed anchors,
FABERGÉ
Presented by Czar Alexander III to his wife, Maria
Feodorovna, c. 1887

A fluted quatrefoil base, elaborately enamelled in the Renaissance style, supports a large natural pearl upon which a perfectly formed egg of rock crystal is held with gold mounts. The base alone is a tour-de-force of the goldsmith's art. Arabesques of translucent blue, green, and red enamel swirl between bands of opaque white enamel dotted with red. Four natural pearls, panels of rose diamonds, and eight brilliant-cut diamonds in black-and-white enamelled mounts complete the extravagant decoration of the base.

Contained within the polished rock crystal shell, banded with gold and diamonds, is an exquisitely wrought Resurrection group: Christ rising from the tomb, flanked by two angels, the figures in the round naturalistically enamelled with opaque colors. This is the first of only two direct references by Fabergé to the religious significance of Easter in the Imperial egg series. The surprise of the Red Cross Egg, presented to the Dowager Empress in 1915, is a miniature triptych of the Resurrection.

The Resurrection Egg is traditionally believed to have been the second egg presented by Alexander III to his wife.

LILIES OF THE VALLEY EGG

Height: 5⁵/₁₆″, open 7⁷/₈″
Marks: MP (Michael Perchin), 56, crossed anchors
Presented by Czar Nicholas II to his mother, Maria Feodorovna, 1898

This confection of pale pink enamel and pearls is one of the most original of Fabergé's creations and, with the Pansy Egg of 1899, one of only two Imperial eggs executed in the then-fashionable Art Nouveau style. The egg is supported on cabriole legs of matte green-gold leaves dripping with rose diamond dewdrops. Nestled in a bouquet of gold-stemmed pearl and diamond lilies of the valley with translucent green enamel leaves, the pink egg is surmounted by a miniature Imperial crown of rose diamonds and cabochon rubies.

A small pearl knob triggers the surprise—a trefoil of Zehngraf's portrait miniatures of Czar Nicholas II and his eldest daughters, Grand Duchesses Olga and Tatiana. A geared mechanism raises the miniatures, which spread fanlike upon emerging from within the egg. They are framed with rose diamonds and backed with gold panels engraved with the presentation date, April 5, 1898.

HOOF EGG

Height: 2⅛", open 3¼"
Marks: MP (Michael Perchin), 56, crossed anchors,
FABERGÉ

Inspired by Russia's rich folklore, this egg with its bizarre cloven-hoof legs of gold was probably presented by the Czarina Alexandra to one of her intimate friends. The surprise is a gold-framed miniature of the Czarina in court dress wearing the famous *kokoshnik* diadem. A small pivot pin enables the miniature to be rotated between the two halves of the bowenite egg. The shell is applied with gold laurel pendants and swags anchored with diamond-set, ruby-centered bows and pearl-headed pins.

CROSS OF ST. GEORGE EGG

Height: 3⁵⁄₁₆", with stand 4⅛"
Marks: FABERGÉ
Presented by Czar Nicholas II to his mother, Maria Feodorovna, 1916

This egg was made of silver as a gesture to wartime austerity. Although smaller and considerably less lavish in the use of precious materials than the pre-war fantasies, this simple egg reflects, nonetheless, Fabergé's unerring sense of proportion and design.

The shell is enamelled an unusual matte opalescent white, underpainted with trellised garlands of pale green laurel framing Order of St. George crosses. A gold ribbon enamelled in the Order's colors of orange and black encircles the egg. Pendant from its bows are two medallions, one the St. George Medal chased in silver with the profile of Nicholas II and the other the Grand Cross of the Order enamelled in extraordinary detail with a miniature of St. George slaying the dragon. Buttons concealed in the ribbons below the medallions trigger springs which cause them to rise. The surprises they reveal are miniatures of the Czarevich Alexis and his father, Czar Nicholas II.

The awarding of the Cross of the Order of St. George by the army particularly moved the Czar.

After 1915 it is the only decoration he wears in most of his photographs and portraits (including the miniature in this egg). After the execution of the Czar and his family, the medal was found hidden in the bathroom of the merchant Impatiev's house where the Imperial family had been imprisoned.

The Cross of St. George Egg was the last egg presented to the Dowager Empress. In a letter to her son after that final Easter before the Revolution, Maria Feodorovna wrote:

> Christ has indeed arisen! I kiss you three times and thank you with all my heart for your dear cards and lovely egg with miniatures, which dear old Fabergé brought himself. It is beautiful. It is so sad not to be together. I wish you, my dear darling Nicky, with all my heart all the best things and success in everything.
>
> Your fondly loving old
> Mama

It was the Dowager Empress's separation from the Czar and his family which made possible her eventual escape from Russia. This egg was the only one she was able to take with her. It was eventually sold at a London auction by her grandson, Prince Vassili Romanov, in the early 1960s.

58

A Catalogue Raisonné
of Imperial Eggs

The following list, illustrated with original drawings, includes all of the known Fabergé eggs presented by Czars Alexander III and Nicholas II to Czarinas Maria Feodorovna and Alexandra Feodorovna. The sizes in inches and millimeters, the workmaster, and the present location are given where known. Since many of the eggs are undated, the years of presentation in some instances can only be conjectured. After the death of Alexander III, his son Nicholas II presented eggs to both his wife and mother from 1895 until 1916. One egg from each of these years—1898, 1905, 1906, 1907, and 1909— has been lost completely, with neither photograph nor description surviving.

Abbreviations
Cleveland—The Cleveland Museum of Art, India Early Minshall Collection
Forbes—The FORBES Magazine Collection, New York
Gray—The Matilda Geddings Gray Foundation Collection, New Orleans
Kremlin—Armory Museum, State Museums of the Moscow Kremlin
Post—The Hillwood Collection, Washington, D.C.
Virginia—Virginia Museum of Fine Arts, Richmond
Walters—The Walters Art Gallery, Baltimore

1886
First Imperial Egg
2½" (64 mm.)
Forbes

1887
Resurrection Egg
Perchin
3⅞" (98 mm.)
Forbes

1888
Danish Jubilee Egg

1889
Egg with Blue Enamel Ribbing
Perchin
4¼" (110 mm.)
Stavros Niarchos, Paris

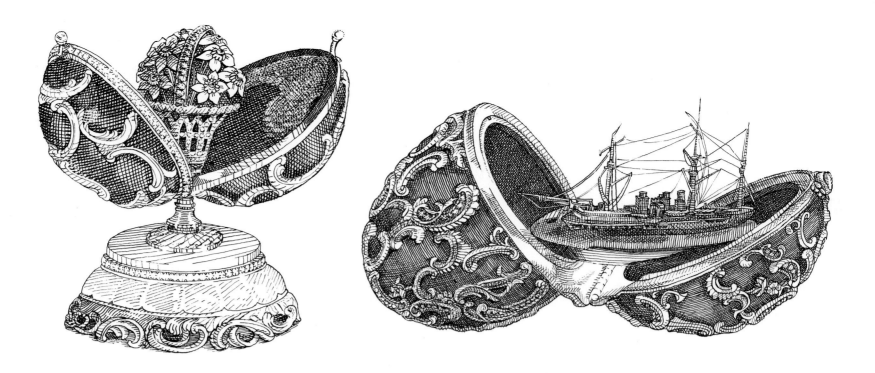

1890
Spring Flowers Egg
Perchin
3¼″ (83 mm.)
Forbes

1891
Azova Egg
Perchin
3⅞″ (98 mm.)
Kremlin

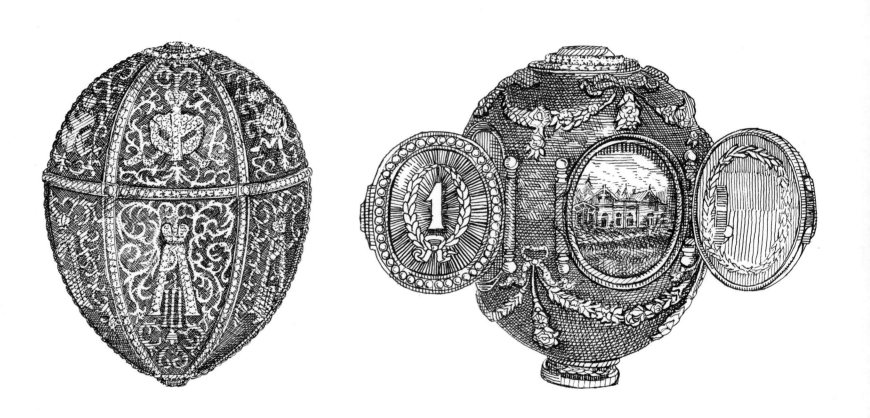

1892
Silver Anniversary Egg
Perchin
3¼″ (83 mm.)
Post

1893
Caucasus Egg
Perchin
3⅝″ (92 mm.)
Gray

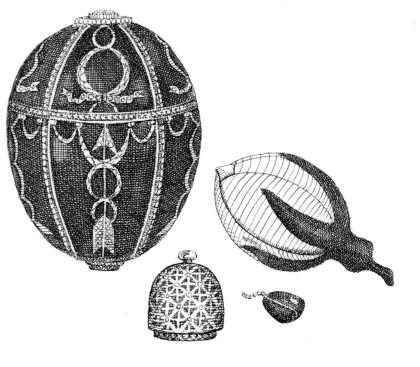

1894
Renaissance Egg
Perchin
5¼″ (133 mm.)
Forbes

1895
Rosebud Egg
3″ (76 mm.)
To Czarina Alexandra

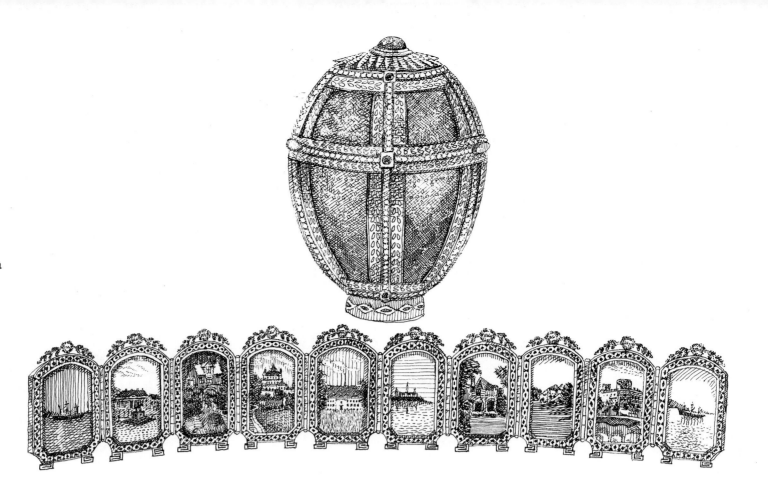

1895
Danish Palace Egg
Perchin
4″ (102 mm.)
To Dowager Empress Maria
Gray

1896
Egg with Revolving Miniatures
Perchin
10″ (254 mm.)
To Czarina Alexandra
Virginia

1896
Blue Serpent Clock Egg
Perchin
7¼″ (185 mm.)
To Dowager Empress Maria
Private Collection, Switzerland

1897
Coronation Egg
Perchin
5″ (127 mm.)
To Czarina Alexandra
Forbes

1897
Pelican Egg
Perchin
4″ (102 mm.)
To Dowager Empress
Maria
Virginia

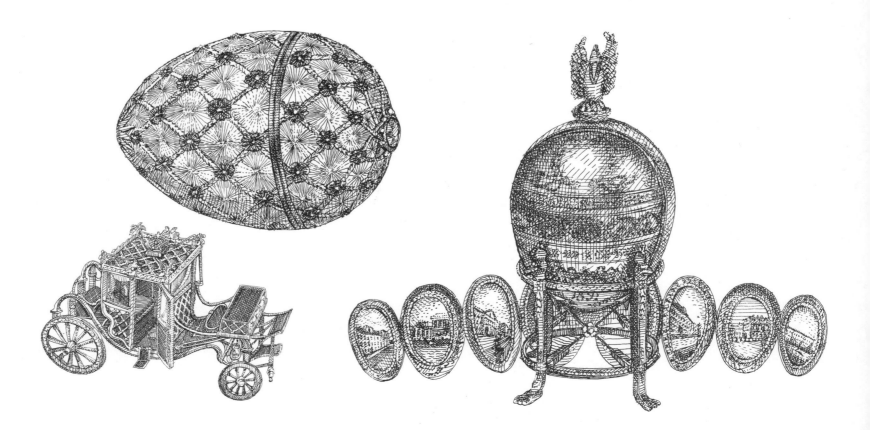

1898
Lilies of the Valley Egg
Perchin
5¹⁵⁄₁₆″ (149 mm.)
To Dowager Empress Maria
Forbes

1899
Madonna Lily Egg
Perchin
10½″ (267 mm.)
To Czarina Alexandra
Kremlin

1899
Pansy Egg
Perchin
5¾″ (146 mm.)
To Dowager Empress Maria
Private Collection, U.S.A.

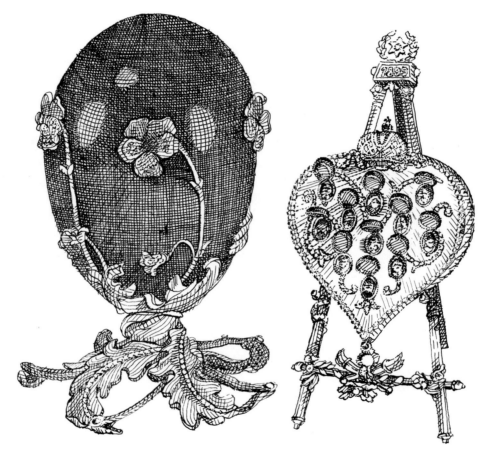

1900
Cuckoo Egg
Perchin
8⅛″ (206 mm.)
To Czarina Alexandra
Mr. and Mrs. Bernard S.
Soloman, Los Angeles

1900
Pine Cone Egg
Perchin
3¾″ (95 mm.)
To Dowager Empress Maria
Private Collection, U.S.A.

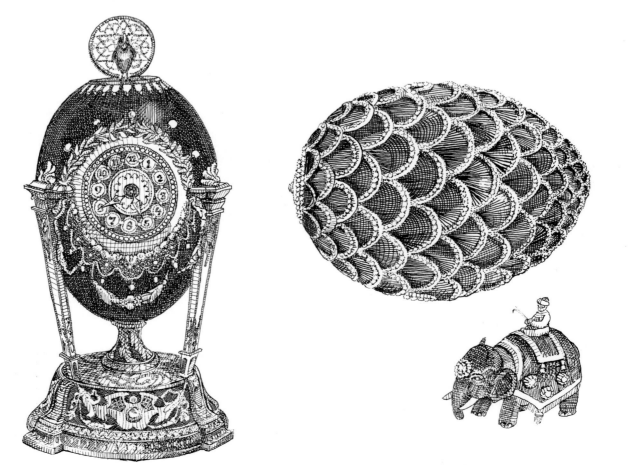

1901
Trans-Siberian Railway Egg
Perchin
10¾″ (273 mm.)
To Czarina Alexandra
Kremlin

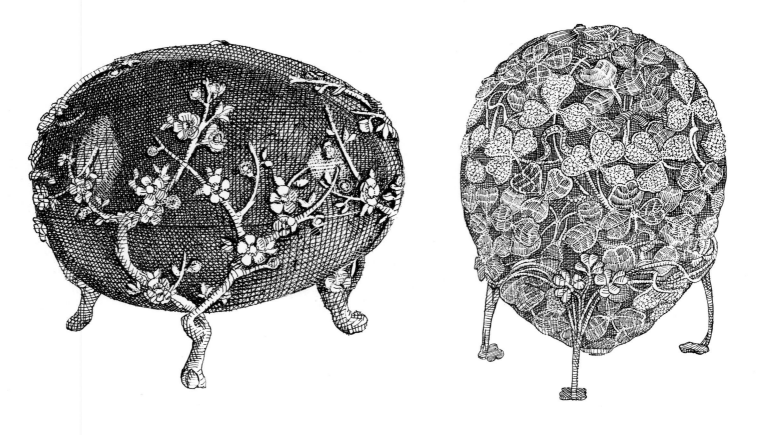

1901
Apple Blossom Egg
Perchin
4⅜″ (110 mm.)
To Dowager Empress Maria
Private Collection, U.S.A.

1902
Clover Egg
Perchin
3⅜″ (85 mm.)
To Czarina Alexandra
Kremlin

1902
Gatchina Palace Egg
Perchin
5″ (127 mm.)
To Dowager Empress Maria
Walters

1903
Peter the Great Egg
Perchin
4¼″ (110 mm.)
To Czarina Alexandra
Virginia

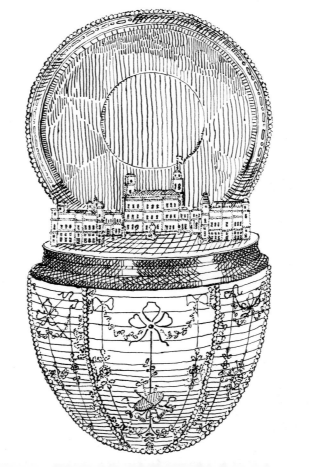

1903
Chanticleer Egg
Perchin
12⅝″ (320 mm.)
To Dowager Empress Maria
Forbes

1904
Uspensky Cathedral Egg
14½″ (370 mm.)
To Czarina Alexandra
Kremlin

1904
**Alexander III
Commemorative Egg**
3¾″ (95 mm.)
To Dowager Empress Maria

1905
Colonnade Egg
Wigström
11¼″ (285 mm.)
To Czarina Alexandra
Royal Collection, England

1906
Swan Egg
4″ (102 mm.)
To Czarina Alexandra
Heirs of the late Maurice
Sandoz, Switzerland

1907
Rose Trellis Egg
Wigström
3¹⁄₁₆″ (77 mm.)
To Czarina Alexandra
Walters

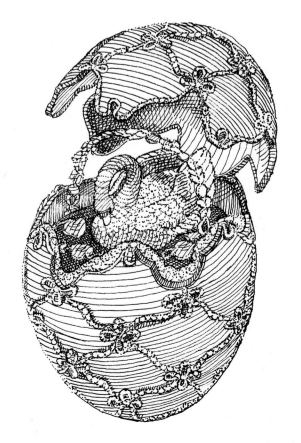

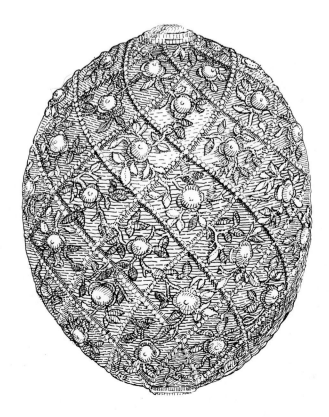

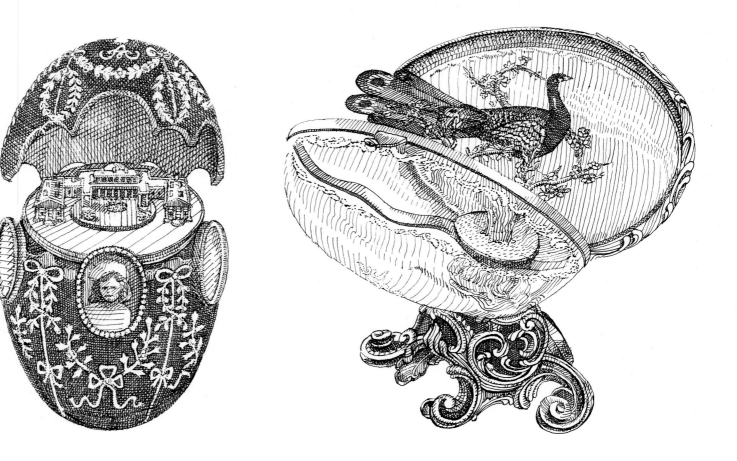

1908
Alexander Palace Egg
Wigström
4¼″ (110 mm.)
To Czarina Alexandra
Kremlin

1908
Peacock Egg
Wigström
6″ (152 mm.)
To Dowager Empress Maria
Heirs of the late Maurice
Sandoz, Switzerland

1909
Standart Egg
Wigström
6⅛″ (155 mm.)
To Czarina Alexandra
Kremlin

1910
Egg with Love Trophies
To Czarina Alexandra
Private Collection, U.S.A.

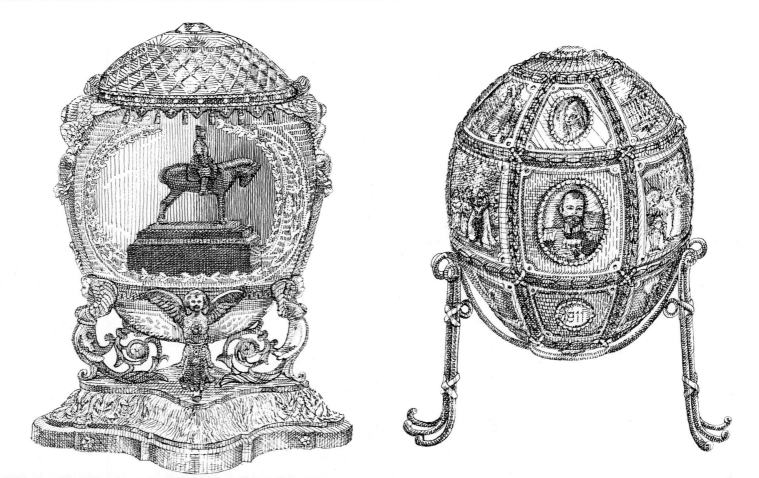

1910
**Alexander III
Equestrian Egg**
6⅛″ (155 mm.)
To Dowager Empress Maria
Kremlin

1911
Fifteenth Anniversary Egg
5⅛″ (132 mm.)
To Czarina Alexandra
Forbes

1911
Orange Tree Egg
10½″ (267 mm.)
To Dowager Empress Maria
Forbes

1912
Czarevich Egg
Wigström
5″ (127 mm.)
To Czarina Alexandra
Virginia

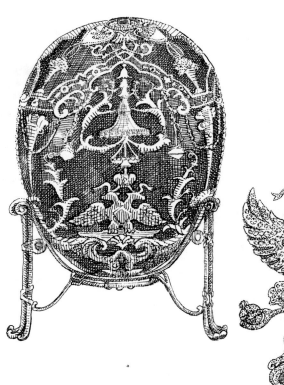

1912
Napoleonic Egg
Wigström
4⅝″ (117 mm.)
To Dowager Empress Maria
Gray

1913
**Romanov
Tercentenary Egg**
Wigström
7⁵⁄₁₆″ (185 mm.)
To Czarina Alexandra
Kremlin

1913
Winter Egg
4″ (102 mm.)
To Dowager Empress Maria
Bryan Ledbrook, Esq.

1914
Mosaic Egg
3⅜″ (92 mm.)
To Czarina Alexandra
Royal Collection, England

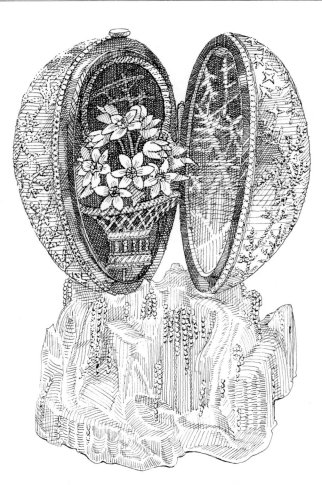

1914
Grisaille Egg
Wigström
4¾″ (120 mm.)
To Dowager Empress Maria
Post

1915
Red Cross Egg with
Resurrection Triptych
Wigström
3⅜″ (85 mm.)
To Czarina Alexandra
Cleveland

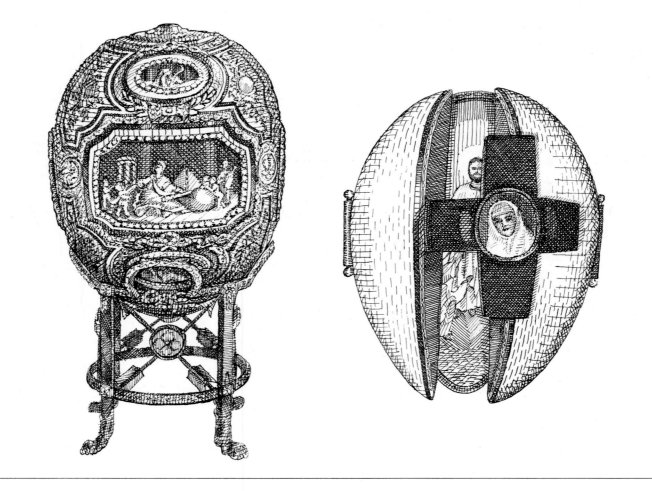

1915
Red Cross Egg with Portraits
Wigström
3½″ (88 mm.)
To Dowager Empress Maria

1916
Steel Military Egg
Wigström
4″ (102 mm.)
To Czarina Alexandra
Kremlin

1916
Cross of St. George Egg
3⁵⁄₁₆″ (90 mm.)
To Dowager Empress Maria
Forbes

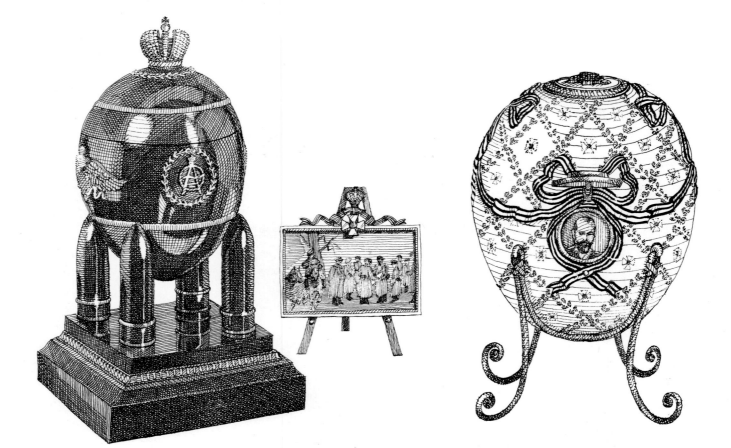